a journey to contentment

navigating through divorce

by e. j. carney

authorHOUSE®

AuthorHouse™
1663 Liberty Drive
Bloomington, IN 47403
www.authorhouse.com
Phone: 1-800-839-8640

Scriptures taken from the Holy Bible, New International Version®, NIV®. Copyright © 1973, 1978, 1984, 2011 by Biblica, Inc.™ Used by permission of Zondervan. All rights reserved worldwide. www.zondervan.com. The "NIV" and "New International Version" are trademarks registered in the United States Patent and Trademark Office by Biblica, Inc.™

Scripture taken from the Holy Bible, New Living Translation are marked (NLT). Copyright © 1996. Used by permission of Tyndale House Publishers, Inc., Wheaton, Illinois 60189. All rights reserved.

Some of the concepts in Chapter 13, "scrape off the barnacles" are adapted from material published in Victorious Christian Living International, SALT Series Version 2.0, Social Area, Copyright © 2006. All rights reserved. Used by permission.

First published by AuthorHouse   02/16/2012

ISBN: 978-1-4685-5313-0 (sc)
ISBN: 978-1-4685-5314-7 (hc)
ISBN: 978-1-4685-5274-4 (ebk)

Library of Congress Control Number: 2012902751

Printed in the United States of America

Any people depicted in stock imagery provided by Thinkstock are models, and such images are being used for illustrative purposes only.
Certain stock imagery © Thinkstock.

This book is printed on acid-free paper.

Because of the dynamic nature of the Internet, any web addresses or links contained in this book may have changed since publication and may no longer be valid. The views expressed in this work are solely those of the author and do not necessarily reflect the views of the publisher, and the publisher hereby disclaims any responsibility for them.

dedication

This book is dedicated to my wonderful friends who read and edited my manuscript. I am grateful for your encouragement and valuable critique. I'd like to say a special thank you to my friend and excellent editor—Valerie Nystrom Paine.

table of contents

foreword

It's been my privilege to watch Edith's journey—her faltering steps, leaps of faith, setbacks and struggles, new relationships and heartaches—all a part of God's unfolding plan.

If you are separated, divorced or going through a divorce, you are not half a person, the flip-side of a coin or part of a picture. You are a whole and complete creative miracle.

This book will give you new insights; renew your faith in a compassionate God and present some concrete ways to "dig" out of the "holes" that keep you from freedom and enjoying life.

May the time you spend reading this book bring you the answers you need and closer to the God who gives them.

Pat Strickland
Christian Educator

Edith Carney will inspire and encourage you all along the way through her new book. She has been a fine church co-worker and friend for many years and I highly recommend her as a writer.

Joseph E. Watkins Jr.
Retired Pastor

preface

Are you going through separation or divorce? Are you feeling anxious and wondering which way to turn? Have you forgotten what contentment feels like? Does your future seem uncertain and bleak? Do you question the promise God gave in Psalm 37:4?

"Delight yourself in the Lord, and he will give you the desires of your heart."

Are you experiencing any of these emotions: shock, hurt, disbelief, confusion, anger or fear? Do you wonder if God knows what you are going through? Do you wonder if He cares? My friend, believe me God knows and He cares.

"O Lord, you have searched me and you know me. You know when I sit and when I rise; you perceive my thoughts from afar. You discern my going out and my lying down; you are familiar with all my ways."

Psalm 139:1-3

You may ask, *if* God knows my thoughts, and even knows when I sit or stand, why is He allowing all of this hurt and turmoil? Why is He allowing my marriage to fail?

I believe that God loves each of us and cares about our lives. He wants us to grow closer to Him and to use these experiences to help others.

This book is based on my journey navigating through divorce. My prayer is that God will encourage and heal you, and give you answers and the direction you need.

the author

chapter one

a safe haven

I was the baby of seven children born to my father, with the last three of us sharing the same mother. Both of my parents had previously been married and divorced. I have memories of my parents screaming, fighting and hitting each other. That's the chaos that filled our home until I was about seven years old when everything changed.

Here's what happened: Our family began attending a little country church and during one evening service Mother and Daddy went to the front of the church to receive Jesus as their Savior. The pastor's wife approached me that same night and asked if I would like to go to the altar and ask Jesus into my heart too. I did want to; so I knelt beside my father and accepted Jesus as my personal Savior.

After that pivotal night instead of waking up to screaming, I would wake up to my mother singing in her wonderful high soprano voice. When I was around eight years old, God healed my father of heart disease and called him into the ministry. Daddy began studying and preparing to meet the requirements to become licensed in the church. He often preached in our local church, visited folks in the hospital and held revivals. I would regularly go with him when he preached and sing special music.

I loved church, singing and quoting Bible verses. Our home was right across the road from a mountain and our house backed up to an irrigation ditch. I remember sitting on the irrigation ditch bank or going up on top of the mountain to sing songs at the top of my voice about how awesome God was. I often walked down to one of the sheds on our farm and would pound on one of the fifty-gallon oil barrels we kept there like it was a piano and sing. After singing most of the hymns I knew and performing my special music, I would preach a real "fire and brimstone" message and give an altar call for the farm animals or any of the neighbors who might be listening. Home was a safe haven for me. I was such a happy young girl. I loved God and wanted to serve Him and do His will.

chapter two

dangerous waters ahead

As I grew older, I was happy and I wasn't looking for marriage. I worked in a local bank, was very involved in church and felt fulfilled. I was training to become an airline communications officer.

Our family had always struggled financially to make ends meet. My mother made most of my clothing out of chicken feed sacks; so when I began earning my own money, I enjoyed buying clothes and matching accessories. One night at church, one of the lay preachers confronted me and told me that I was causing my Christian brothers to stumble because I was wearing beige colored high heels with open toes and open heels. He said that a godly woman should only wear closed in pumps and they should be either black or white. There were a lot of rules at this church. We didn't go to movies, dances or even roller skating.

One day as I was heading to lunch, I passed by one of the local department stores where the store owner was standing outside. He asked me if I had a boyfriend. He said I was pretty and smart and should be dating. It is funny how someone's words can plant a thought in your mind. Shortly after that I was on my way to a Wednesday night church service with another girl. She saw an old classmate headed towards a local drive-in restaurant. She believed he was a perfect match for me and suggested that we go check it out instead of going to church. By the time we arrived at the drive-in, the classmate had a couple of girls in the car with him. However, he asked them to leave and invited us to go to a drive-in movie with him.

We had been classmates but had never shared a romantic interest in one another. We had very different backgrounds and except for our intellect had very little in common. We began dating and in a couple of months we got engaged. I quickly started feeling uneasy about marrying him so I ended our relationship. In my journey, I've learned that when I don't feel God's peace about something, I better not do it.

Several months passed and one morning my phone rang. It was my former fiancé. He *said* he had accidently called me; he meant to call someone else. As we talked, he invited me out for dinner that night so I went. He asked me to reconsider his proposal of marriage. He had the rings in a safety deposit box and said if I did not marry him that he would have the rings made into a ring for his father. Rather than going to dinner as planned, he took me home, promising to return the next day to hear my decision. Sure enough he returned the next day, placed an engagement ring on my finger and we set our wedding date to take place in six weeks.

rough winds blowing

I asked five different ministers to perform the ceremony including my father, but none of them would agree to officiate at the wedding. They said we would be "unequally yoked together." I thought it wasn't right for them to judge whether or not my future husband was a Christian. I was now determined to marry him. As I look back now, I see my actions as not only a sign of immaturity but ultimately rebellion and sin. I went against biblical teaching and my father's wishes by rushing into this marriage.

Besides I figured I *couldn't* back out of the engagement even if it was wrong. My father had taught us that a man was no better than his word. If you say you are going to do something, then you better do it. I said I would marry my fiancé so I was going to keep my word. Since then I have learned that if we promise to do something that isn't right or God's will, we must reconsider and back out of the situation if possible. Unfortunately I didn't back out of my decision so we endured twenty very rocky and unhealthy years together.

My Christian upbringing taught me that marriage was the first institution God established back in the Garden of Eden. In the beginning there wasn't a suitable partner for Adam. In Genesis 2:18-24, God acknowledges this fact and says, *"It is not good for the man to be alone. I will make a helper suitable for him."* So the Lord caused the man to fall into a deep sleep; and while he was sleeping, He took one of the man's ribs and closed up the place with flesh. Then God made a woman from the rib He had taken out of the man, and He brought her to the man. When Adam awoke he said, *"This is bone of my bones and flesh of my flesh; she shall be called 'woman,' for she was taken out of man."*

From the beginning, before there even were parents, God told man to form a new family unit and establish a different residence with his wife. New couples need privacy to develop closeness and intimacy. This is the reason why a man needs to leave his father and mother and be united to his wife. God knew what was best and how to make a healthy, happy relationship.

eye of the storm

Our honeymoon was very precious. We were both naïve and fearful. Our marriage counseling had consisted of about ten minutes the night before our wedding with the pastor and his wife. The pastor counseled my husband while the pastor's wife counseled me. Her counsel was "the first night you spend together will be painful as you consummate your marriage. Remember we must stand pain for those we love". Not much help there.

We were both so nervous after the wedding that our mouths were dry. We must have stopped at every drive-in restaurant we passed to get something to drink.

My husband was very gentle and loving on our honeymoon. I could not have asked for anything more except for the fact that he called his family every night. He would go into great detail as he told them how wonderful it was to have intimacy of marriage. I felt the intimacy between husband and wife should be private. I did not want to share this part of my life with anyone especially not my in-laws!

hurricane force winds

We were married for about a week when my husband's father passed away. Feeling his immediate responsibility to his mother and younger sister, my husband asked me for an annulment. I was shocked! I did not know what to do. I went to my brother, who was my husband's best friend, and sought his advice. He told me my place was with my husband and that I must help him and his family get through these trying times. So instead of getting an annulment or beginning our own home, we moved into my mother-in-law's house.

She was treated like the "Queen". I continued my job as well as doing most of the cooking, laundry and housework for my husband, mother-in-law and sister-in-law.

We did not have the privacy a young married couple needs. Our intimacy was being shared with my husband's mother and sister. It had a very harmful effect on our marriage.

Once in the early days of our marriage, my husband came into the kitchen where my mother-in-law and I were. He said he did not like my dress and began ripping it off me. I was very embarrassed standing there in front of his mother with both of them laughing.

tidal wave of rejection

About a year after our marriage, my husband told me that he needed to get some life insurance. He asked me to contact an insurance agent to come to the house and talk with him. I was pregnant with our first child and thought my husband wanted to care for me and his child if something were to happen to him. However, when the insurance agent arrived, my mother-in-law invited him in. She and my husband discussed the policy with me being in another room. I felt like an outsider. My husband made his *mother* the beneficiary. I realized then that he wanted to care for his mother rather than his pregnant wife.

My husband came from a dysfunctional family, had a bi-polar personality disorder, volatile temper and was suicidal. I had never dealt with this type of situation before and really didn't know how to handle it. In those days no one talked about mental problems or suicide, not even to their relatives. I tried to be a supportive wife. I prayed a lot for our marriage. I had always been good at fixing things. Surely I could fix my marriage and my husband. I was convinced that I could make my husband happy.

spawning a storm

Why did *you* get married? Did you get married to get away from home? Were your friends all getting married? Did you want to fix your fiancée? Were you in a rebellious stage or have wrong motives at the time of your marriage?

I see that my rebellion against God and my father spawned a terrible life storm. My motives were wrong. I am grateful that God forgives our sins when we ask Him. He forgave my rebellion. There are, however, consequences for rebellion and sin and I have suffered my share.

I encourage you to face the waves that rebellion has caused and ask God for forgiveness so you can move on to calmer waters and toward healing.

chapter three

the watery depths

Is your relationship going down? You are not alone. Divorce is widespread even in churches. There are literally thousands of shipwrecked individuals who are in the same situation that you are. They never thought their lives would be broken through separation and divorce either.

I remember when I realized that my marriage was falling apart. Nothing seemed right. I loved my husband. I loved my children. Yet, there was so much stress in our home that you could cut it with a knife. My husband went from guilt and anger, to depression and suicidal tendencies. He talked about what "a bear of a job" he had and how unhappy he was. He described his working atmosphere as a "snake pit" or an "alligator pond". Since he was so miserable at work, I tried to make him happy at home. I took on all the responsibility for his happiness which caused more harm than good. I couldn't satisfy him no matter how hard I tried. I felt like I was walking on egg shells to keep the peace. I never knew what might send him into depression or an angry rage. I couldn't satisfy him sexually either. He looked outside of the marriage to satisfy his sexual desires.

I was so stressed out that I finally lost it. I had always been a stable and calm woman but one day I picked up a pancake spatula and began beating the kitchen counter and screaming at the top of my voice. I called my husband every awful name I'd ever heard. My husband had never seen me come unglued before and I think he thought I was losing my mind. The really sad part of the incident was that my children heard it all. When a local pastor showed up unannounced at our door, one of our teen-age sons sadly told him that it was not a good time to visit. No, it wasn't a good time.

What was I going to do? We continually hurt one another. Many times I would drive to a local park to "talk to the squirrels" just to obtain some type of sanity. Observers probably thought I was nuts!

We were both seeing counselors. My husband had gone to counseling for a year to help him get over his depression and suicidal tendencies. Once a month, I talked with his counselor. We each had a different perception of our situation. The counselor said he didn't know which story to believe; they were both so believable, yet entirely opposite.

I no longer respected nor trusted my husband. I decided that I should take responsibility for my life and happiness. So after years of stress, anxiety and enduring my husband's unfaithfulness, I left home and took our daughter with me. My husband and I shared custody of our teen-age sons. Deep down in my heart I hoped separation would change things and that we would get back together again. However I must admit it felt great getting away from all the anxiety and pain in our home and experience a little peace.

man overboard

We were separated for a year and my husband was dating others. He wanted me to come home, but under his demands which included letting him do as he pleased and continue to be unfaithful. One night he called and asked me to come over to listen to his three propositions. First, could we be friends? I said "yes". Second, could we be friends on an intimate basis? I said "no". Lastly, my husband asked if I would move back in with him that very day as his wife. He had filed for divorce a couple of months earlier. I told him "No, we should let the divorce go through. However, if he wanted to date me after the divorce was final so we could rebuild respect, love and trust again, I would consider a remarriage". He was not agreeable to *my* proposal. As I was leaving, we went to the mailbox and got the mail. Our final divorce decree was in the box.

I got in the car and as I turned toward home, I felt *peace* in the car. It was like God was saying, "IT'S OKAY, IT'S TIME TO MOVE ON". My husband left that very day and drove to another state to pick up a woman he had met earlier. She moved in with him and eventually became his wife. Our relationship had finally gone down to the watery depths and was no more.

chapter four

headed off course

Have you wondered if you did the right thing by ending your marriage? Did you feel like you were way off course? I sure did. Although I felt peace when our divorce was final, I soon began to experience doubts. I was tormented by thoughts like: Maybe I should have moved back into our home. Maybe I should have tried a little bit harder. Maybe I should have forgiven one more time. Maybe I should have gone to biblical counseling and tried to change myself. Maybe, maybe, maybe.

The fact was it no longer mattered if I had done the right thing or not. I was divorced. I couldn't go back. I had to go forward. Worry, doubts and regrets don't fix anything.

I've come to understand that there are only three things you can do about your past: **repent** if you've sinned, **forgive** if you've been hurt and finally **thank God** for all of it.

Perhaps you've made more mistakes than you care to think about, here's the Good News: God can forgive your sin—this includes divorce and the sins and mistakes which preceded it. Simply tell God what you've done and accept His forgiveness. That's the *repent* part of dealing with the past.

> *"God makes you alive with Christ. He forgave us all our sins."*
>
> Colossians 2:13

While you're at it, why not be bold and even *thank* God for your past—the good, the bad and the ugly?

> *"Always giving thanks to God the Father **for everything**, in the name of our Lord Jesus Christ."*
>
> Ephesians 5:20

Once you've repented, forgiven and thanked God, you will be able to stop worrying about the past and move forward. Forgiving my ex-husband was so freeing that I dedicated Chapter 13 to how to completely forgive.

Spending time with my Heavenly Father helped me make it through my divorce and it got me back on course. I couldn't have done it without Him. Like a sailor can get his bearings from the North Star, focusing on God will help you navigate through the rough waters too.

chapter five

chart the journey

Wouldn't it be great to not only survive your divorce but actually come through it spiritually, psychologically and emotionally with flying colors? Divorce doesn't have to shrivel or forever scar you. I can prove it to you. Begin charting your journey. In other words, start keeping a journal.

Writing in a journal is a lot like sharing with a friend or confidant. You won't be judged for what you say and you don't have to be concerned about what you write. There are no rules—messiness, typos, poor writing are all OK. Write about your thoughts, feelings and desires. Write your prayers. Record whatever comes into your mind and then talk to God about what you have written. God cares about you and He is a safe place to pour out your heart.

> *"Trust in him at all times, O people; pour out your hearts to him, for God is our refuge."*
>
> Psalm 62:8

Keeping a journal can help you gain clarity, perseverance and the courage you need to carry on through difficult times. Journaling can reduce stress, release pent-up emotions, help you see the big picture and identify your successes and mistakes. Journaling encouraged me as I went through divorce. I remember reading my journal about what had happened and how I felt a few months earlier and I was able to see how much I had grown since then and even laugh about some of my entries.

Use the 31 Days Journal at the back of this book to get started.

Journaling will help you track your progress, like a ship's log charts a journey, and will show you that you are growing and that things are getting better.

chapter six

navigate three passageways

On your journey through divorce, you will most likely go through three passageways or stages. The first one is usually *shock*; you can't believe that this is happening to you. You never thought that your castle would crumble or your ship would go down. You thought you would be happily married for life.

As you navigate through this passageway, your emotions might be all over the place—feeling deeply hurt, confused and depressed are common. At times you may even feel anger towards yourself, spouse and God.

As I finally accepted that my divorce was final, I entered into the second passageway or the second stage of divorce which was *adjustment*. I realized things were different now; I'd gone from being two to being just one. My income, social life, days and nights were all different. Now I was making decisions on my own. It was quite an adjustment.

Then I entered the third passageway which was *growth*. I was growing into a different person. I discovered I could do things I never thought I could do. I was stretched by having to manage the finances, home and work responsibilities and take care of my children. I was growing and so were my children. It was scary wondering if they would turn out alright.

My daughter *did* drop out of high school just six weeks before graduation but later went on to college earning her bachelor's and master's degrees. She is happily married, the mother of three wonderful children and involved with church and Christian school.

My sons also went through hard times but they too became fine responsible adults. I can't say that I didn't have a lot of stress and experience anxious moments during their teen-age years. They tried my nerves with various dangerous activities like driving cars way too fast and other youthful stunts but both of them went on to have honorable careers in the military and are now married with wonderful children and good jobs.

With God's help, I was able to keep my sanity and let my children know how much I loved them and how proud I was of each of them as I went through the three passageways of divorce—shock, adjustment and growth.

chapter seven

commander of the vessel

There's a famous picture of a young man with his hands on the wheel of a ship with Jesus standing behind him. It's called "God is My Co-pilot". That was my problem! I needed God to be the Pilot not the copilot. My way wasn't working. Yes, I loved God but He wasn't the Commander.

Have you been doing things your own way too? How has it been working for you? He needs to be in charge and at the helm. Come to Him and He will show you the direction you need to go. You can trust Him.

"Come to me, all you who are weary and burdened, and I will give you rest. Take my yoke upon you and learn from me, for I am gentle and humble in heart, and you will find rest for your souls. For my yoke is easy and my burden is light."

Matthew 11:28-30

Putting God in charge of your life is a wonderful thing because He loves you. In fact he wants to be your Heavenly Father. Do you have complete assurance that you are God's child? If you are not sure that you would go to heaven when you die, I would encourage you to take the following steps:

First, you must realize you are a sinner.

"For **all** have sinned and fall short of the glory of God."

Romans 3:23

"All" includes you and me. Second, believe that Jesus Christ took the punishment for your sins.

"But God demonstrates his own love for us in this: While we were still sinners, Christ died for us. Since we have now been justified by his blood, how much more shall we be saved from God's wrath through him! For if, when we were God's enemies, we were reconciled to him through the death of his Son, how much more, having been reconciled, shall we be saved through his life!"

Romans 5:8-10

Third, confess your sins to God and receive His forgiveness.

"Then I acknowledged my **sin** to you and did not cover up my iniquity. I said, 'I will **confess** my transgressions to the LORD'—and you forgave the guilt of my **sin** . . ."

Psalm 32:5

You could say a prayer like this: "God, I have thought, said and done wrong things. I need Your forgiveness. Thank You, Jesus, for taking my punishment and dying in my place. I receive Your forgiveness. Please be the new leader of my life."

christening

If you prayed that simple prayer or one like it, you are named as one of God's children and God is your Heavenly Father. I encourage you to start reading a Bible daily—begin in the book of John then read Romans. The Bible is one of the ways that God gives direction.

Find a good church home and attend some of the small Bible study classes so you have a safe place to ask your questions.

Talk with God every day. Don't know how to pray? Talk to God like you would a best friend or a loving father. Find a time when you can shut out distractions and just be with God. He will tell you how much He loves you and give you direction for your life.

"Call to me and I will answer you and tell you great and unsearchable things you do not know."
Jeremiah 33:3

"Whether you turn to the right or to the left, your ears will hear a voice behind you, saying, 'This is the way; walk in it.'"
Isaiah 30:21

The more you talk to God the better you will get to know Him and recognize His voice. You usually hear Him speaking through the Bible verses you read or in your thoughts. As you learn to hear God's voice, keep in mind He will never tell you to do something that contradicts the Bible. As you get to know your Heavenly Father, you will become a much happier, positive person—that makes you a much better spouse. If you choose not to marry again, knowing your Heavenly Father will give you peace in your singleness.

One of my best times for prayer is traveling to work. I thank God for sending His Son to die on the cross for my salvation. I thank Him for the beautiful country He has provided for us. I thank Him for the rain, the sunshine, the clouds, even the fog and snow. I also thank Him for my family and friends. I pray for those who have hurt me. I ask Him for strength to get me through the day and to help me to be a positive, happy person. I ask Him to help me to please Him at work and wherever I may be during the day.

> "We have this hope as an **anchor** for the soul, firm and secure . . ."
>
> Hebrews 6:19

Even though it was distressing raising three children alone, when I put Jesus in charge, He showed me which way to go and I had peace.

chapter eight

discover treasure

It's been said that the greatest commandment could be summed up like this: Love God *completely*, love others *compassionately* and love yourself *correctly*. God wants us to love Him with our whole being and thoughtfully care for others but what does it mean to love yourself?

Loving yourself *correctly* means that you understand how special you are to God—you are fully loved and accepted by Him. You are special! You are a treasure! That's healthy self-esteem. Healthy self-esteem is very important for any relationship. My favorite scripture is:

"For you created my inmost being; you knit me together in my mother's womb. I praise you because I am fearfully and wonderfully made; your works are wonderful, I know that full well. My frame was not hidden from you when I was made in the secret place. When I was woven together in the depths of the earth. Your eyes saw my unformed body. All the days ordained for me were written in your book before one of them came to be."

Psalm 139:13-16

God loves you so much that He designed a plan for your life *before* you were born! You have value and worth.

"So God created man in His own image, in the image of God He created him; male and female He created them."

Genesis 1:27

How awesome it is that God created man, male and female, in His own image! What a wonderful act of God. If He created us in His image and accepts us as His kids, then we should have a healthy dose of self-esteem.

Healthy relationships start when you are secure in God's love for you. You don't need anyone else's love for your security. If you have a low self-esteem or an incorrect love for yourself, I encourage you to reread or even memorize the above scriptures.

Start saying, out loud if possible, what God says about you. Like: *"I am deeply loved by God, completely forgiven because of Jesus, fully pleasing to my Heavenly Father, totally accepted by God and complete in Christ."* I guarantee it—that will build your self-esteem!

chapter nine

star gaze

The Bible states *"where there is no vision, the people perish."* You need to have a vision for your life and future. Look up and dream a new dream!

One of my dreams was to be involved in ministry. I had the privilege of serving on the singles staff of a wonderful church. I am grateful to both the Senior Pastor and the Singles Minister for believing in me and granting me the privilege of being on staff.

You can begin dreaming a little by making a couple of lists. Get some paper and a pen. Turn on some good up-beat music. Write the changes you want to make in your life—spiritually, psychologically, socially, physically, financially, in your marriage and as a parent or grandparent. These could include such things as:

- Change careers
- Move to a different part of the country
- Build a new relationship
- Get out of debt
- Spend more time with kids
- Purchase a new house or car
- Take a vacation
- Get into better physical condition
- Start going to church

Make a second list of your talents—list the things you love to do. These could include abilities like:

- Good home-maker
- Accurate with numbers and finances
- Skilled gardener
- Talented writer
- Gifted singer or artist
- Experienced teacher
- Knowledge of computers and technology

As you look over your lists, they could trigger what you really want out of life and help you begin "dreaming" about your future. God has such good plans for you. Get a vision of what those plans are by talking to Him.

> *"'For I know the plans I have for you,' declares the LORD, 'plans to prosper you and not to harm you, plans to give you hope and a future.'"*
> Jeremiah 29:11

How do you achieve your dreams? They might seem too difficult to obtain, like reaching for the stars. Remember the Bible says, *"I can do all things through Christ who strengthens me."*

It is wise to plot a course or map out the steps you must take to achieve your dreams.

> *"Those who are wise will shine like the brightness of the heavens, and those who lead many to righteousness, like the **stars** for ever and ever."*
>
> Daniel 12:3

The next chapter describes how to set and accomplish goals.

chapter ten

map it out

In the previous chapter, you did a little dreaming. So where do you want to go? What do you want to be doing a year from now? What do you want to be doing five or ten years from now? How do you get there? You need to plot your course and map it out. SET GOALS!

Goal setting is probably the most vital skill a person needs to be successful. When you become a goal setter, and think, write, and talk about your goals on an ongoing basis, your level of performance and achievement improves dramatically—almost immediately. You begin to feel more successful and thereby obtain a better self-image which prepares you for good strong relationships.

When you set goals, you get direction and focus your energy. You end up accomplishing more in less time because you are spending less time spinning your wheels or headed in the wrong direction. Why, then, do so few people set goals?

avoid the reefs

There are several obstacles or reefs which thwart people's goal setting efforts. First, the majority of people don't understand the *importance* of goals. Secondly, they don't know how to set and achieve them. Third, they get talked out of them—every time they set a goal, somebody tells them they aren't smart enough, talented enough or determined enough to achieve it. Finally, they fear *failure*. "What if I don't reach my goal? I may as well not even try."

fear of failure

Throughout the years, I have found that failure has actually been beneficial to me. I learned what **not** to do and became much better at making good decisions.

I remember the story of Thomas Edison developing the electric light bulb. Concerning his many "failed" attempts, he said: "We now know a thousand ways not to build a light bulb." We certainly have benefitted from Mr. Edison's failed attempts and ultimate success! We have to be willing to risk failure. There is no way we can realize our full potential unless we have failed at times. Eventually we learn the lessons necessary for us to go on to our greatest achievements.

types of goals

There are different types of goals and different ways of setting them. I refer to goals in terms of *upward* (spiritual, praise, worship, submission to God), *outward* (business, career, community service, relationships with peers and others) and *inward* (personal goals relating to self and family).

Before setting goals, our priorities should be checked. Ask yourself: Is it pleasing and acceptable to God? Am I considering my family responsibilities? Is self-justification, selfish motivation and self-gratification behind my goals?

> *"So we make it our **goal** to please Him whether we are at home in the body or away from it."*
>
> 2 Corinthians 5:19

> *"**Whatever you do**, do it all for the glory of God."*
>
> 1 Corinthians 10:31

It's important that we set goals which are consistent with our desires and still pleasing to God.

write your goals

The few people who *do* set goals seldom set them effectively because they don't crystallize their thoughts in writing.

> *"Then the LORD replied: 'Write down the revelation [vision] and make it plain on tablets so that a herald may run with it.'"*
>
> Habakkuk 2:2

This is why I encouraged you to make lists in the last chapter and even earlier when I suggested that you start journaling. Take advantage of the journal at the back of this book. It takes some effort to put your goals into writing but I strongly encourage you to do so. A goal is not a goal until you specifically define how you are going to get there.

short and long term goals

Earlier I divided goals into three categories: *upward* or spiritual, *outward* or business and careers, and *inward* or family and personal. I further divide goals into three time periods: short-term, medium-term and long-term. After writing down my goals, I define the tasks or steps required to reach each goal. You may prepare your list of goals in much the same manner.

Begin by making a list of your lifetime goals—between now and the end of your life. Don't stop to think about it; just write everything down. Be specific. Setting lifetime goals will give you focus for your life and be a constant reminder as to why you are doing everything else in your life. These will be your long-term goals.

To achieve your long-term goals, begin to make short term goals that support your long term goals. Being conscious of your short term goals will help you stay motivated because once you achieve a short term goal you have a sense of accomplishment that will make you press forward in achieving your other goals. For example, suppose one of your long term goals is to be healthier. To do this, you must exercise weekly, maintain healthy eating habits and consume a limited number of calories so you can maintain your ideal weight. These actions will serve as your short-term goals.

Be specific as you make a list of your short range goals (one week to six months).

Keep your list of goals where you can review them regularly. Keep them updated. You may want to put your goals on three by five cards and keep them in your appointment calendar. As you accomplish each goal, cross it off and update your list.

be realistic

Set realistic goals but make them challenging. Many people fail to reach their goals because they are neither realistic nor challenging. Assign tasks which will enable you to achieve your goal.

don't give up

You may think you don't have what it takes to reach certain goals. You may feel you aren't as smart as someone else and therefore, give up. Don't give up! Everyone has many average talents and abilities, but every one also has the ability to achieve excellence or make an outstanding accomplishment in at least one specific area.

> *"For we are God's workmanship, created in Christ Jesus to do good works, which God prepared in advance for us to do."*
>
> Ephesians 2:10

You were created by God. You are His masterpiece and designed to accomplish something very special. One of your goals should be to discover what that is and to determine your potential area of excellence.

Do you remember the story about a man who went far away to find a special diamond? Years later he discovered that what he thought was only coal in his own backyard was really a diamond field. The point of the story is: everything you need is probably very close at hand.

think on these things

Setting goals and thinking continuously about them raises your self-esteem and moves you toward realizing your full potential!

e.j. carney

> *"Finally, brothers, whatever is true, whatever is noble, whatever is right, whatever is pure, whatever is lovely, whatever is admirable—if anything is excellent or praiseworthy—think about such things."*
>
> Philippians 4:8

Best wishes on dreaming your dreams, mapping out your goals and fulfilling the desires of your heart!

> *"In the last days, God says, 'I will pour out my Spirit on all people. Your sons and daughters will prophesy, your young men will see **visions**, your old men will **dream** dreams.'"*
>
> Acts 2:17

chapter eleven

flotsam & jetsam

As you navigate through divorce, you will discover there are things in your life that need to change. Difficult times often reveal negative patterns of behavior and unhealthy thoughts and insecurities—all things that slow you down or hinder your progress. We need to get those things out of our lives.

Flotsam is floating wreckage of a ship or its cargo. *Jetsam* is part of a ship, its equipment, or its cargo that is purposefully cast overboard or jettisoned to lighten the load in time of distress.

> " . . . let us throw off everything that hinders and the sin that so easily entangles, and let us run with perseverance the race marked out for us."
>
> Hebrews 12:1

Throughout my life, I had *always* taken responsibility for everyone's happiness and making sure everyone's needs were met. I believed that I was called to be the "peace maker." For years, I failed to see how my "mothering" did more harm than good. During my divorce, I recognized that my actions had actually hindered my husband and kept him from changing. I had to stop taking responsibility for his emotions and actions. I needed to throw my control and taking unnecessary responsibility for others overboard.

cast off fear

I also needed to overcome a few fears. Perhaps you have some of the same fears that I had or others like: Will you make it? What if you get fired? Will your kids be harmed for life or will your family and friends turn against you? What if the car breaks down and you don't have enough money to pay for repairs?

If you've had some of these fears, you *can* and *will* make it. I did and you can too! The road will get easier and easier.

hoist the sails

Here are some things that blew fresh wind in my sails, encouraged me and relieved my fears:

First, I found a good church—one with a good singles ministry. Find a church that loves you even when you are not at your best and get involved in one of the ministries of the church.

I set aside time every day for some sort of devotions—like Bible study, prayer, singing, and reading biblical-based books.

I started thanking God for everything including my hurts and praying for those who had hurt me.

I went to divorce recovery workshops and after my healing and recovery participated in conducting the workshops. If there is a Divorce Recovery Workshop, Prescription for Mending, Fresh Start, Mending Broken Hearts or a Divorce Care seminar in your area, try to attend one.

I kept a daily journal. This will be most valuable to you as you are growing through your divorce. When you think you haven't made any progress, you can go back to the beginning of your journal and see that you have.

I listened to Christian praise music and watched uplifting sermons on TV.

I started paying attention to my diet, exercise, rest and stress levels. I had to change my poor life style of eating junk food, skipping meals and staying up too late.

I started helping others. Find someone who is hurting more than you are and help them. When you help others, you spend less time thinking about yourself and all of those "what if" fears.

I stood on this promise. Hoist your spiritual sails and catch the winds of the Spirit.

"I can do everything through Him who gives me strength."
Philippians 4:13

relationship fears

Do you have a fear of being in a relationship and loving again? I did. During the years following my divorce, I dated several men who either talked about marriage or asked me to marry them. I was afraid to love again. I was terrified of marrying a man like my former husband. I had to keep my focus on God and ask for His direction in relationships.

> *"There is no **fear** in love. But perfect love drives out **fear**, because **fear** has to do with punishment. The one who **fears** is not made perfect in love."*
>
> 1 John 4:18

No one knows better than God what is best for your life. He knows if you should remarry and if so who that person would be. However friends sometimes think they know what is best for you and what type of person you should marry.

I had friends who loved me and wanted me to be happy. They knew what I had gone through in the past. They believed in me and trusted God had a very special plan for my life. They didn't want me to settle for second best. I loved and appreciated them for that.

At times it was confusing when other friends gave me their views on who I should or shouldn't marry. They would tell me not to marry one particular man because he was "too old" and not "spiritual enough." Then they didn't want me to marry another man because he was "not ambitious enough." They gave me their opinion whether I wanted it or not.

You, too, may have friends who are trying to decide for you. You may resent them interfering in your life, but weigh their words. Take the good advice and throw out the rest. Spend a lot of time in prayer. Listen to your Heavenly Father and He will show you what to do.

chapter twelve

time in dry dock

Maintenance of ships is important for the safety and life of the vessel. The maintenance activity, or dry dock, includes working on the interior, exterior and machinery of the ship. How's your time in dry dock, or recovery, going? Are you tired of being worked on? Do you just wish you could get on with your journey and leave the pain behind?

First, we don't go around or over or under the pain. We must go *through* it. The journey to healing and wholeness is a transformational journey because we are changed in the process. Therefore the goal is not to be on your way again or get back to the way you were. The goal is to grow and come out of "dry dock" better than you were before. It's been said, "Trials can make you better or they can make you bitter." It depends on how you handle your decisions, thoughts and pain.

If you try to ignore or refuse to face the pain, bitterness and unforgiveness will affect your body, soul and relationships.

> *"See to it that no one misses the grace of God and that no* **bitter** *root grows up to cause trouble and defile many."*
>
> Hebrews 12:15

how long in dry dock

I've learned that not everyone comes out of "dry dock" or recovers at the same rate of speed. Don't compare yourself with anyone else. You are special and unique! God made you that way. Trust in Him to carry you through each stage of maintenance.

Part of the time in "dry dock" will include repenting of your mistakes in the marriage. Trust Him to forgive you. Remember you *have* and you *will* make mistakes but God loves you. He will use everything you have gone through for good—so that you will be whole and become more like Jesus.

> *"And we know that in all things God works for the good of those who love him, who have been called according to his purpose. For those God foreknew he also predestined to be conformed to the likeness of his Son, that he might be the firstborn among many brothers."*
>
> Romans 8:28-29

the tears

There will be many a tear, but someone once told me that tears are God's way of washing away the poison. The ability to shed tears, to weep, seems to be a uniquely human response to pain. Tears cleanse and heal. Don't be afraid to cry and show your emotions. God cares about your pain and tears. Notice what Psalm 56:8 says in the New Living Translation Bible:

"You keep track of all my sorrows. You have collected all my tears in your bottle. You have recorded each one in your book."

Your tears are so precious to God that He collects them in a bottle and records each one in His book.

no emotions

Even though I now understand tears are okay, I got tired of crying and began shutting down my emotions until I didn't feel anything. I blocked out a lot of the pain which also caused me to forget some of the enjoyment of life. That reaction isn't unusual. Sometimes when we experience overwhelming pain and loss, we may tend to go numb. Going numb can be a small mercy which enables us to go on with life—however don't fall into the trap of staying there and never feeling again.

phases of dry dock

No matter what phase of "dry dock" I went through, I could see healing and growth taking place in my life.

I went through a phase of worrying whether or not my husband would be all right but I discovered he could function just fine without me. I grew as I released the responsibility I felt for him.

I went through a phase of getting back in the "singles" lane again. I had married when I was barely nineteen years old so it had been a long time since I was single. During this phase, I grew as I ventured out to meet new people.

I went through a phase of feeling the need of a relationship when my former husband had a new woman in his life. I am so glad God protected me from getting married too quickly. Too many of my friends married before they really knew the individual or before both of them had been healed from their previous marriages. Therefore, the baggage from the previous experiences was carried into the new relationship, and in most cases, things did not go too smoothly.

slips to avoid

Unfortunately some of the groups I visited, encouraged infidelity. Only they didn't call it infidelity. They called it "helping each other get through tough times" and "enjoying meeting each other's normal, physical need". After a man would "wine and dine" a woman a few times, he felt he was entitled to some "payback" or sexual favors. The women were just as aggressive as the men in seeking a "good time". They rationalized their behavior because "everyone was doing it".

God understands our weakness and He will forgive us. However He still expects us to obey Him and His Word. The Bible teaches us to run from sexual immorality which is sex outside of marriage.

> *"But among you there must not be even a hint of **sexual** immorality, or of any kind of impurity, or of greed, because these are improper for God's holy people."*
> Ephesians 5:3

Sexual immorality is sin and has many painful consequences like guilt, shame and possibly disease.

> *"Flee from **sexual immorality**. All other sins a man commits are outside his body, but he who sins sexually sins against his own body."*
> 1 Corinthians 6:18

Sex creates a bond, regardless of how casually it is entered into, and therefore can cause problems in a future marriage.

"Do you not know that he who unites himself with a prostitute [or anyone other than his wife] is one with her in body? For it is said, 'The two will become one flesh.'"

1 Corinthians 6:16

Be strong and don't submit to sexual sin. However, if you have, STOP it now, ask God to forgive you and remember you belong to Jesus.

"Do you not know that your body is a temple of the Holy Spirit, who is in you, whom you have received from God? You are not your own; you were bought at a price. Therefore honor God with your body."

1 Corinthians 6:19-20

I am glad for the phases I went through and how they helped me grow but I am certainly happy not to go through any of them again.

chapter thirteen

scrape off the barnacles

Have you forgiven your ex-spouse? Or are you holding on to your offenses, grudges and unforgiveness toward him/her?

"Be kind and compassionate to one another, forgiving each others, just as in Christ God forgave you."

Ephesians 4:32

These things are the "barnacles" of life. Barnacles attach themselves to the hull of a ship and cause all kinds of problems. Their presence increases friction, diminishes speed and increases fuel consumption. They need to be scraped off. It's the same with grudges and unforgiveness. They slow you down and make life so much harder. Their presence will affect you and your relationships.

> *"Therefore, since we are surrounded by such a great cloud of witnesses, let us throw off everything that hinders and the sin that so easily entangles, and let us run with perseverance the race marked out for us."*
>
> Hebrews 12:1

Forgiving those who have hurt you is *vital* for recovering from divorce and *essential* if you enter into a serious relationship again.

seventy-seven times

You may find that you need to go through forgiveness more than once. I have asked God to forgive me for my part in the divorce and I've forgiven my ex-husband for the hurts, the emotions and the ramifications I received from him. I have also asked my ex-husband for his forgiveness.

Just about the time I think I have done everything I need to do to be free from unforgiveness, another ramification of the divorce comes to light and I get upset all over again. That's when I realize that I need to forgive one more time and scrape off another barnacle.

> *"Then Peter came to Jesus and asked, 'Lord, how many times shall I forgive my brother when he sins against me? Up to seven times?' Jesus answered, 'I tell you, not seven times, but seventy-seven times.'"*
>
> Matthew 18:21-22

how to fully forgive

The following process comes from the "Forgiveness" chapter in the SALT Series by Victorious Christian Living International. It has been extremely helpful to me. I wept as I heard this teaching and I spent two hours the next day to work through these steps.

Use this exercise to forgive those who have hurt you. On a separate piece of paper, answer questions 1-5. *There may be more than one offender that you need to forgive.*

1. Who do you need to forgive? What is your offender's name?

2. What did he/she do or not do that hurt you?

3. How did you feel about it? (*list all of your emotions*)

4. How did his/her actions affect you in the 7 areas of life? (spiritually, psychologically, socially, physically, financially, martially, parentally)

5. What were your wrong or sinful reactions to the offense?

Now forgive your offender using the following steps:

Step 1—Forgive the Offense

Choose to forgive the person for the wrong that he or she did to you. Jesus paid for the sins of the world when He died on the cross—even the sins committed against you. You are choosing to no longer hold him/her guilty for the offense. You might pray something like this, *"Heavenly Father, I choose to forgive (name the person who offended you) for what he/she did to me (be specific and name the offense) I believe the blood of Jesus covers their sin."*

Step 2—Forgive the Hurt

After you forgive the offense, take the time to forgive all the hurt feelings you have experienced. *"I choose to forgive him/her for the feelings that I experienced because of the offense. I believe the blood of Jesus covers these hurts."* (Be specific and list the emotions you experienced.)

Step 3—Forgive the Ramifications

Now choose to forgive the offender for how the offense affected all other areas of your life. *"I choose to forgive him/her for all the ramifications (list them) caused by the offense. I believe the blood of Jesus covers all the areas that were affected."*

Step 4—Confess Your Sinful Reactions

"Lord, I acknowledge that I have sinned too. I confess and repent of my sinful reactions (be specific). Thank You that the blood of Jesus covers my sins and that I am forgiven."

This process of forgiveness is between you and God. The other person doesn't have to ask first, deserve it or ever know you did it.

Please note: As you confess your sinful reactions in step 5, you may see that *you* need to ask forgiveness from the person you have wronged. Simply admit your wrong actions to him/her, don't make excuses, and then ask for forgiveness without expecting any particular outcome.

forgive yourself

I often hear people say we need to forgive ourselves. If we could forgive ourselves however, we wouldn't need Jesus our Savior. Only Jesus' blood is enough for forgiveness. The *real* problem is that we are judging ourselves for our failures and the divorce. In essence we are taking God's place.

*"There is only **one lawgiver and judge** . . . ."*

James 4:12

Admit to God that you have been trying to take His place and repent of judging yourself. When you forgive others and ask for forgiveness from God and those you have offended, you have scraped the barnacles of life off of your vessel. You can continue your journey unhindered.

chapter fourteen

caught in a whirlpool

One of the areas that might pull you under in a divorce is your finances. Examining where you are financially is the first step to breaking free from this treacherous whirlpool.

My children and I were financially comfortable with a nice standard of living in those days before the divorce. My husband and I were the usual two professionals working full time and bringing in two nice paychecks. Even though we were unhappy together and our marriage had become a very unhealthy one, we both wanted the best for the family.

Since neither of us wanted to take everything financially from each other, I did not secure the help of a lawyer. Probably not very smart but I reasoned that at least our emotions would be spared from court battles. I moved into a condo and took one of our cars, some of the cookware, dishes, linens, other household goods and my bi-weekly paycheck. I did not receive or give child support or alimony.

Our boys were old enough to drive, so we agreed that they would stay with their dad but would be able to come to my home as often as they wished. I retained full custody of our daughter. Soon after the separation, our oldest son went off to college and I got full custody of the other son.

the spin cycle

I wanted to make sure my children got the material things they needed, which included clothes, cars and college. It was much too easy to obtain bank cards, department store credit cards and gas cards. When the children needed anything or I thought I needed a new suit for an interview so I could get a better job to better care for myself and the children, I just charged on the credit cards.

No problem at first. I paid my bills on time and developed an excellent credit rating for myself. Soon other card companies began to send me those nice, little notes saying, "Because of your excellent credit rating, you have been approved for our card at a limit of $2000." Wow! I signed my name and sent a paper back and pretty soon another card would arrive.

pulled under

The children needed a new pair of shoes, college tuition paid or a plane trip to a friend's wedding. What should I do? Charge it! Pretty soon, I would get another nice little note saying "Because of the excellent manner in which you have paid, we are raising your credit limit to $5000." Fantastic!

Get the picture? You have taken care of your family, your friends and yourself, but your finances are out of control! You have been sucked into the world's debt based whirlpool or economy.

This is the story of how I unwittingly let my finances get out of control. There are other people who are compulsive shoppers and live beyond their means. They try to fill a need with material possessions and indulge in frivolous purchases, trips, meals and toys in order to impress others.

> *"Let no debt remain outstanding, except the continuing debt to love one another, for he who loves his fellowman has fulfilled the law."*
> Romans 13:8

If *you* are in debt, let me encourage you to do something about it. Get your finances back under control. How? First if you don't have a monthly budget, start one right now and stick to it. Second spend *less* than you earn. If you will do these two things, you will get out of the debt you're in and experience peace of mind. Will Rogers said, *"If you find yourself in a hole, stop digging."*

Use the Monthly Budget Worksheet in Appendix 1: The first step in preparing a budget is to determine and record your total income. Be sure to include in the total all income you take home from work as well as income from other sources such as stock dividends, child support and alimony.

Next write down all of your expenses. Don't leave anything out; you must get a true picture of where you are financially. Don't forget to include those stops at the coffee shop, lunches out and money you give your children.

There are also many good resources available like Victorious Christian Living International's *SALT Financial* book, Dave Ramsey's *Financial Peace* and Willow Creek's *Good Cents* to name a few.

Now here's the bottom line. Look at what you have recorded. If your expenses are greater than your income, your budget is out of control. You are caught in a financial whirlpool! DON'T ALLOW YOURSELF TO CONTINUE TO GROW DEBT!

chapter fifteen

stay afloat

It certainly was tough for me financially from the beginning of my separation and for many years thereafter. Living on credit and getting into debt started off easy but in the end it produced death. If this is the case for you too, it is time to recognize your need to get out of debt.

The previous chapter focused on how my budget got out of control. One reason was because I obtained too many credit cards. Another problem was not having a budget—at least not a written one. Proper management of a budget is much like goal setting. It must be written out to really produce the proper effects. *"Write the vision"* Habakkuk tells us.

Do you have a written budget? Do you know how deeply in debt you are? I was quite surprised to find out how much I actually owed when I did an inventory and prepared a written budget.

There are numerous people doing seminars on budgeting and getting out of debt. I mentioned a few in the last chapter. Many of the seminars are free through local churches. Take advantage of these seminars. Your time is all you invest. Listen, analyze and then take what would be helpful for your particular case.

For me to get of debt, I had to do the following:

First, I had to have the desire to be financially free. I had to believe God wanted me to be out of debt and figure out how to get my priorities straight.

Second, I set realistic goals. I made reducing my debt one of the goals in my short-term and long-term.

Third, I made a list of all the companies/people I owed and how much I owed them. This is included in the written budget. I had to be honest and write down every expense.

Forth, I calculated my monthly income and monthly living expenses.

My fifth step was to start tithing 10% of my income to the church I attended or other charities. At first I wondered if God would notice my charitable contributions. However, I marveled that God caused blessings to flow as I became a faithful steward of what He gave me. I encourage you to obey God's plan for prospering.

> *"Give, and it will be given to you. A good measure, pressed down, shaken together and running over, will be poured into your lap. For with the measure you use, it will be measured to you."*
>
> Luke 6:38

The next step was to start saving or investing 10% of my net income. Five percent was currently being invested into a Thrift Savings Plan at work. I added an additional 5% to a separate investment program. I made this a bill just like any other.

I had to stop spending more than I was making so I cut up the credit cards—all of them. If I had just put them away, it would have been too easy to pull them out again when I thought I needed something.

Finally, I requested a reduced repayment schedule from my creditors. It is a good way to produce extra money you need to balance your budget. Below is an example for you.

AN EXAMPLE—DEBT REDUCTION WORKSHEEET

Accounts Owed	Total $ Due	Monthly Payment	Reduced Payment
Master Card	460	25	16.50
Department Store	330	20	13.20
Bank Loan	2,205	115	77.90
Car Loan	3,000	156	102.96
Totals:	**5,995**	**316**	**210.56**

In this example, I figured how much I could afford to pay each month, and then I wrote to each creditor. I explained that I couldn't make the original monthly payment but a payment of the reduced amount would be paid every month until the debt was paid off. It is important to let the creditor know that the debt will be paid.

I paid off the smallest debt I owed first. This gave me a feeling of accomplishment. When I experience success, it is easier to continue being successful. My self-esteem goes up and I feel good!

I used the amount from paying off the smallest debt to help pay off the next smallest debt or the debt with the highest interest rate. I continued the process until all debts were paid. In the process, I made myself accountable to someone who prayed for me.

This is what the Bible has to say about being in debt.

"This is also why you pay taxes, for the authorities are God's servants, who give their full time to governing. Give everyone what you owe him; if you owe taxes, pay taxes; if revenue, then revenue; if respect, then respect; if honor, then honor. Let no debt remain outstanding, except the continuing debt to love one another, for he who loves his fellowman has fulfilled the law."

Romans 13: 6-8

"The rich rule over the poor, and the borrower is servant to the lender."

Proverbs 22:7

If we are in debt, we are not as free or in control of our life as we want to be. I certainly don't want anyone but God to control me. This helped to reinforce the importance of becoming debt-free to me.

It is never easy to get out of debt once you are there, but with God, all things are possible, even getting out of debt!

chapter sixteen

stuck in the doldrums

The doldrums are when the winds totally disappear and trap sail-powered boats for long periods of time. When the winds are gone, the sea actually has no swells, on a clear day the color of the sky is reflected in the water. At night with no clouds or moon, it feels like you are floating in space. The term "doldrum" is derived from "*dold*" an archaic term meaning "stupid".

Do you feel like everyone around you has found their own special person but you're stuck in the doldrums? Floating in space, going nowhere, feeling foolish? Do you question why God hasn't brought the right person into your life yet? Why is it taking so long? Or do you wonder if God plans for you to be single the rest of your life? I asked many of those same questions.

One of my best friends wrote me a letter saying she was getting married again—after her *second* divorce. I came apart! She was getting married *again.* It had been almost nine years since my divorce and I still wasn't remarried.

Sure I had dated several men and even considered the idea of marriage but after I got to know them a little better, my feelings changed. There wasn't anything wrong with them. I just gave myself enough time to get to know them—their quirks, habits and personalities.

I didn't like this process. I felt like I was sitting around in the doldrums.

get to know each other

I've met a lot of couples who got married before they really knew each other. It wasn't surprising that before too long they were having problems. As a result of couples spending more time together, unpleasant qualities in each individual were exposed, like selfishness and control. This discovery produced feelings of disappointment and disillusionment and lead to conflict. Since they didn't know how to resolve conflict God's way, the marriage would end in separation or divorce.

God wants to provide for you so don't be in such a rush to fulfill your own wants and desires. Trust Him.

> "For the pagan world runs after all such things, and your Father knows that you need them. But seek his kingdom and these things will be given to you as well."
> Luke 12:30-31

"Delight yourself in the Lord and He will give you the desires of your heart."

Psalm 37:4

"And my God will meet all your needs according to His glorious riches in Christ Jesus."

Philippians 4:19

while in the doldrums

If you are in the doldrums and don't have anything better to do, why not identify some of the causes of your failed marriage. Was it sin on your part like it was in mine? If it was, have you asked for forgiveness? Sometimes it's difficult to admit that we have sinned. We would rather say we made a mistake. But if we admit our sin, we take the first step toward turning our lives around. We can be healed from the hurts and go on to find a healthy relationship. Jesus came to free us from the penalty of sin and to free us from the power of sin.

"If we confess our sins, He is faithful and just to forgive us our sins and to cleanse us from all unrighteousness."

1 John 1:9

Be patient in the doldrums. Concentrate on getting your own act together. Work on knowing and talking to your Heavenly Father. One day the fair winds will blow and you, too, can find love again.

chapter seventeen

avoid the sirens' song

During a separation and divorce, you are very vulnerable even if you don't feel like you are. Be prepared to face many temptations. If you surrender to them, you will be robbed of many blessings and may experience much hurt and pain.

> *"The thief does not come except to steal, and to kill, and to destroy. I have come that they may have life, and that they may have it more abundantly."*
>
> John 10:10

In the Odyssey, the Sirens sing a song so irresistible that none who hear it escape. Circe warns Odysseus of the danger and tells him how to avoid it. He must plug up his men's ears with beeswax, and have himself tied to the mast, if he wishes to hear it:

> Square in your ship's path are Sirens,
> Crying beauty to bewitch men coasting by;
> Woe to the innocent who hears that sound!
> He will not see his lady nor his children in joy,
> Crowding about him, home from sea;
> The Sirens will sing his mind away on their sweet meadow lolling.
> There are bones of dead men rotting in a pile beside them
> And flayed skins shrivel around the spot.
> Steer wide; keep well to seaward;
> Plug your oarsmen's ears with beeswax kneaded soft;
> None of the rest should hear that song.
> But if you wish to listen,
> Let the men tie you in the luger,
> Hand and foot, back to the mast, lashed to the mast,
> So you may hear those harpies' thrilling voices;
> Shout as you will, begging to be untied,
> Your crew must only twist more line around you
> And keep their stroke up, till the singers fade. (Book 12, 41-58)

life boat

The Sirens in this story are very similar to the temptations you face in the world. The only way to resist the Sirens was to close your ears to their song and run! The Bible says:

> **"No temptation** has seized you except what is common to man. And God is faithful; he will not let you be tempted beyond what you can bear. But when you are tempted, he will also provide a way out so that you can stand up under it."
>
> 1 Corinthians 10:13

Here are some of the temptations you may face and good ways to overcome them.

Temptation: Continuing to take responsibility for your ex-spouse or other adult's happiness and wellbeing.

The Way Out: Give your ex-spouse to God and take responsibility for your own life and actions.

I joined an organization for single parents. It was a good organization but there were plenty of opportunities to give into temptation. For instance, often these events were 'wine and cheese' chat groups or dances. Although I am glad I never gave into this temptation, what could have been just a really nice time frequently ended in sin. Participants would drink too much and then paired up to go home with each other. More victims swept away by the "Sirens' song".

satan's pirate ship

Satan's goal is to raid and steal from you. He wants to destroy you and your family. Beware!

> "The thief [Satan] comes only to steal and kill and destroy;
> I [Jesus] have come that they may have life, and have it to
> the full."
>
> John 10:10

Temptation: Overindulging in alcohol and sexual immorality.

The Way Out: Ask God for His help and look for the way out. Escape the situation.

> "Everything is permissible for me—but not everything is
> beneficial. Everything is permissible for me—but I will not
> be mastered by anything. Food for the stomach and the
> stomach for food—but God will destroy them both. Flee
> from sexual immorality . . ."
>
> 1 Corinthians 6:12-13, 18

63

scrub the deck

Just because everyone else is doing wrong, doesn't make it right. The Bible says there is pleasure in sin for a *season*. That season doesn't last forever. Soon the pleasure turns to shame and guilt.

Temptation: Trying to escape loneliness through drugs, alcohol or mindless activities.
The Way Out: Spend time with God. Get together with some good friends.
I saw many people use alcohol as their friend. It led to depression and ruined their lives.

> *"Don't be drunk with wine, because that will ruin your life. Instead, let the Holy Spirit fill and control you."*
> Ephesians 5:18 (NTL)

If you are lonely, find some good friends to have dinner with, go to a movie or for a walk. Most importantly remember God hasn't left you.

> " . . . God has said, 'Never will I leave you; never will I forsake you.'"
> Hebrews 13:5

pier (peer) pressure

Temptation: Blindly doing whatever others want you to do.

The Way Out: Weigh your friend's advice and ask God for direction. I had a friend who was involved in a group that he thought would help me so he offered to pay my way to one of their conferences. The very first thing the speaker said was not to tell anyone what was talked about or what occurred during the conference. Their message, which completely left God and Jesus out, asserted that everything we need for life is inside of us. They turned out to be one of the New Age associations. After attending a couple of sessions, I became very ill and knew that God did not want me there. I quickly got myself away from this group.

> *"Jesus answered, '**I am the way** and the truth and the life. No one comes to the Father except through me.'"*
>
> John 14:6

Be careful of such groups. In fact have nothing to do with them. Jesus is the only way to real life not self.

Temptation: Self-focus. Thinking only of your own wants and needs at the expense of your children.

> *"People will be **lovers of themselves**, lovers of money, boastful, proud, abusive, disobedient to their parents, ungrateful, unholy, without love, unforgiving, slanderous, without self-control, brutal, not lovers of the good, treacherous, rash, conceited, lovers of pleasure rather than lovers of God—having a form of godliness but denying its power. **Have nothing to do with them.**"*
>
> 2 Timothy 3:2-5

The Way Out: Take care of your children's needs—for love, direction and provision.

If you have minor children at home, consider what affect dating and other social activities (that don't include children) may have on them.

> *"If anyone does not provide for his relatives, and especially for his immediate family, he has denied the faith and is worse than an unbeliever."*
>
> 1 Timothy 5:8

maintain the ship

Temptation: Not taking care of your body.

The Way Out: Take care of your health. Remember your body belongs to God.

Brush your teeth, get cleaned up, drink water, eat wholesome foods and exercise—these disciplines seem simple but when you are struggling just to get through the day you might need to be reminded.

here's the quay (key)

Have fun as you grow and learn to be single again but always put Jesus first. He will be your companion, friend and lover. Satan comes to rob you but Jesus came to bring you abundant life. He is the way out of temptation and away from the Sirens' song.

chapter eighteen

welcome on deck

As you have been growing through your divorce, you have gone to new places and accomplished things you may have never thought you could. In addition you have welcomed new people into your life and begun building fresh relationships. Good for you!

While I was involved in the Singles Ministry, I conducted several surveys on dating. I asked both men and women what qualities were on their "perfect mate" wish list. Some lists were short and succinct; some could fill a book.

Are you ready to start dating again? Consider developing the following six things because they appear on most people's list.

the "perfect mate" wish list

1. **Confidence:** Confidence attracts. Have an accurate appraisal of yourself—your strengths and talents. Take an honest look at the things you don't like about yourself and work on correcting them.

2. **Sense of Humor:** Having a good sense of humor has many benefits. It helps you see the lighter side of life, it brings happiness to everyone you meet and you look better when you are smiling.

"A happy heart makes the face cheerful . . ."
Proverbs 15:13

3. **Looks:** Yes, looks *are* important but not everyone is attracted to the same look. Put some effort into finding the right hairstyle and wearing clothes that look nice on you. Be clean and smell good. Those simple things go a long way.

4. **Acceptance:** Everyone is unique. Celebrate the differences in others instead of trying to change people. It feels good being accepted.

5. **Communication:** Learn to be a good listener and how to express your thoughts, feelings and wants clearly.

6. **Financial Stability:** There's no question that people who have their finances in order are a lot more appealing than those who are deeply in debt. Take the necessary steps to financial obedience.

How did you do? Need to work on anything?

low pressure system

When you are ready to start dating again, take it slow and establish a friendship first. Get to know each other through church settings, group outings and friends.

Go on low pressure dates like meeting over coffee or for lunch or:

- Attend outdoor community concerts. You'll find many communities that offer some sort of outdoor concerts for the sake of the community. Some of them charge a little for the privilege of listening to great music while others offer the event for free.

- Festivals, fairs and open air markets. These can provide many hours of enjoyment and entertainment. They are mostly outdoor events held in the daylight hours and are very public. This means they are great first date material for nervous daters meeting the first time as well as those who know each other but not all that well. These dates are low pressure because there isn't a prevailing sense of romance in the air so you're free to get to know one another, walk, talk, and enjoy the sights and sounds.

- Miniature golf, bowling, roller skating, ice skating, go kart riding, cross country skiing, downhill skiing, skateboarding, snowboarding or surfing. These are great because they are fun, can be done in groups, and you can talk while you're doing them.

- Spend the day at the zoo, aquarium, museum or art gallery. Make a plan to have fun.

biblical qualities

The Bible lists many fine qualities which we should cultivate in our lives and look for in others but the number one factor should be that you and your future spouse are Christians.

- Commitment to Biblical beliefs and values and lives a lifestyle consistent with those beliefs and values.

"Do not be yoked together with unbelievers. For what do righteousness and wickedness have in common? Or what fellowship can light have with darkness?"

2 Corinthians 6:14

- Ability to listen and communicate thoughtfully.

"My dear brothers, take note of this: Everyone should be quick to listen, slow to speak and slow to become angry."

James 1:19

- Not ruled by emotions or feelings.

"Refrain from anger and turn from wrath; do not fret—it leads only to evil."

Psalm 37:8

- Builds you up and doesn't tear you down. Treats you with respect.

"Do nothing out of selfish ambition or vain conceit, but in humility consider others better than yourselves. Each of you should look not only to your own interests, but also to the interests of others."

Philippians 2:3-4

- Acts responsibly and admits when they have made a mistake.

"Therefore confess your sins to each other and pray for each other so that you may be healed. The prayer of a righteous man is powerful and effective."

James 5:16

- Concerned for others. Respects their parents.

"'Honor your father and mother,' and 'love your neighbor as yourself.'"

Matthew 19:19

- Dresses and acts modestly.

"I also want [men and] women to dress modestly, with decency and propriety . . ."

1 Timothy 2:9

- Is a person of integrity and is honest.

"Kings take pleasure in honest lips; they value a man who speaks the truth."

Proverbs 16:13

Ask yourself, how well do I fit this description?

roles of husband and wife

If you remarry, you need to follow God's plan for marriage. He created marriage and wants marriages to be healthy and strong. Men and women are perfectly designed to fulfill the roles of husband and wife.

God created husbands to be the spiritual leader. If the man follows God's commandments, he becomes a loving leader not a dictator. God didn't give us dominion over each other. Men can be loving but not lead. They can be leaders but lead in a way that is not loving. Spiritual leadership takes both. This is a big responsibility.

"Husbands, love your wives, just as Christ loved the church and gave himself up for her"

Ephesians 5:25

Wives need to be the good support. If the woman follows God's commandments, she will be a loving support to her husband. Her wisdom, intuition, skills and sensitivity will help her husband and make the marriage strong.

"She brings him good, not harm, all the days of her life."

Proverbs 31:12

heed the lighthouse

Proverbs warns us of the perils of associating with the wrong kinds of people and it illuminates the qualities of a good friend. People who choose to disregard what the Bible says about friends, relationships and marriage may one day wish they had never welcomed that person aboard and into their life.

chapter nineteen

a journey to contentment

What does contentment really mean? Webster defines contentment as the state of being contented. He defines content as: Not desiring more than what one has; satisfied. He makes a statement—content oneself by working hard or with the thought that work is the best cure for worry. Contented is defines as: Satisfied with things as they are.

high and low tides

I was certainly not satisfied with things the way they were. In fact, I was miserable. I was confused, hurt, felt rejected and anxious. However I've learned that a sailor doesn't become skilled in calm seas.

Today, I can read back through some of my journals and laugh. I can see how worried and unsettled I was. Today, I am satisfied with things as they are. My children grew up and are all doing fine. I paid my bills and finally became debt-free. Best of all, I know I am "God's Child" and that He knows what is best for me. I continue to do interesting and challenging activities. I was satisfied in my present state of singleness, possibly because I knew I could marry again if I chose. The actions I chose would determine my state of happiness, fulfillment and contentment.

During the past several years, I have had numerous dreams. Many of these dreams have been fulfilled and have aided in my becoming a more contented and happy person. I continue to have dreams, set goals, and am expecting a happy, challenging future.

You too, can dream and see those dreams fulfilled. How?

"If they obey and serve him, they will spend the rest of their days in prosperity and their years in **contentment.***"*
Job 36:11

Joy and contentment come from loving and obeying God.

Here's the secret: No person and *no* situation has to change for you to be content. Contentment isn't a faraway island or a planet out in space. It's available to all of us—right here and right now—whatever the circumstances.

"I have learned the **secret of being content** *in any and every situation, whether well fed or hungry, whether living in plenty or in want. I can do everything through him who gives me strength."*
Philippians 4:12-13

chapter twenty

land ho

". . . let us run with patience the race that is set before us, looking unto Jesus the author and finisher of our faith."
Hebrews 12: 1-2

As I have journeyed through extreme stress, anxiety, separation, divorce, forgiveness, building new relationships and generally getting on with my life, my viewpoints have changed in many respects. I believe that we have a race to run but must take the time to fully recover before moving into another marriage after a divorce. I also believe that God wants to use all of our experiences, both good and bad, to help others down the road.

"Praise be to the God and Father of our Lord Jesus Christ, the Father of compassion and the God of all comfort, who comforts us in all our troubles, so that we can comfort those in any trouble with the comfort we ourselves have received from God."

2 Corinthians 1:3-4

After a thirteen year journey of being single, I sighted land. God gave me the desires of my heart!

"Delight yourself in the Lord and He will give you the desires of your heart."

Psalm 37:4

A dear lady in my Sunday school class told me that I should put an advertisement in a Christian Singles newsletter. I thought that was the craziest idea I had heard in a long time. I thought it was dangerous and just plain ridiculous! After all, I had met several men that I could marry if that was my ultimate goal. I believed that if God had a "special man" for me out there that He would bring him to me or vice versa. I didn't have to go out looking, especially in the "want ads."

A year went by and this same woman again told me that I should put an "ad" into a Christian Singles newsletter. This time she gave me the address. I acquiesced and sent in my advertisement which read as follows:

F150303—Edith-Southwest-early 50's, Government Manager, MBA, 5'5", White, silver hair, brown eyes, non-smoker/nondrinker. Nazarene background. Aged Mom lives with me. Can travel. Interested in godly, positive, non-smoker, who can enjoy an attractive, full-figured, intelligent woman. Friendship for now-perhaps marriage in time. Enjoy church, communication, gospel music, travel, walking, reading, movies, open to other activities and learning. Am warm & affectionate, but abide by God's commands.

I figured if I said my "aged Mom lived with me" that would scare away a lot of men I would not be interested in dating. I also wanted whoever read the ad to know that I followed God's commandments with no compromise. That would rule out all those with values different from mine. After sending my advertisement, I went to the altar at my local church and asked God to give me the "desires of my heart." He answered my prayer as was promised.

> *"Ask and it will be given to you; seek and you will find; knock and the door will be opened to you."*
>
> Matthew 7:7

About a month later, I received the men's advertisements from the Christian Singles newsletter and came upon the following:

M1746630-Burt-West Coast-MA degree, Anglo, Non-smoker/ nondrinker, a dedicated, educational administrator, late 40's, even-tempered, considerate, faithful, seek a good-humored, marriage-minded lady who loves the Lord, appreciates the Pentecostal experience, & really enjoys gardening. My other interest includes discussing world affairs, travel, and bird watching. I've never been married, am shy, so please be gentle. Prefer to correspond with a lady from west coast or southwest.

This man met my main criteria: Christian, non-smoker, educated and the right age. I was also struck by the phrase "never been married am shy, so please be gentle." I immediately wrote to him. After corresponding for several months, Burt invited me to visit him for a weekend. He said that he would put me up in a local motel which helped me to know that it would be "honorable" to visit him.

During this visit, I met one of Burt's sisters and her family. He also met my older brother and his family. We were each in our own way getting confirmation that the relationship was right. I knew by the end of that first weekend that I was going to marry

Burt. By our second weekend visit the following month, he knew it too. We were engaged a couple of months later and married by the end of the year.

From the very beginning of reading Burt's ad and through our wedding, I felt complete peace and knew that this relationship was made by the Lord. How wonderful it is to be in God's will with the man of my dreams!

We found communication to be one of the primary keys for developing a great relationship. As we went through our courtship, we wrote down questions for each other on three by five cards. When we saw each other, we would ask our questions. The answers led to other questions and by the time our wedding date arrived, we knew each other quite well.

We wrote our wedding ceremony and developed a list of marriage principles. We wanted a God centered marriage because we both believed that to be the main ingredient in making a good marriage. We put a lot of time in preparing our marriage principles. We developed them, prayed over them and finally finished them. *These principles are working for us and they are included in Marriage Principles in Appendix 2.*

drop anchor

God has truly given me the desires of my heart through my marriage to Burt. I have come to a place of rest and contentment.

Regardless of what stage in your journey you may be in, God's promises are for you too. Pursue Him. He will give you the desires of your heart!

appendix 1

monthly budget worksheet

INCOME:

Salary	$_____
Investment Income	$_____
Other Income	$_____

Total Income: $_____

EXPENSES:

Contributions	$_____
Savings/Investments	$_____
Housing (mortgage or rent)	$_____
Utilities:	
Gas	$_____
Water	$_____
Electricity	$_____
Phone (house and cell)	$_____
Cable/Internet	$_____
Sewer	$_____
Garbage	$_____
Auto (payment)	$_____
Maintenance	$_____
Gas	$_____
Food	$_____
Personal items	$_____
Medical	$_____
Insurance	$_____
Clothing	$_____
Education	$_____
Recreation	$_____
Pet food and care	$_____
Credit card payments	$_____

Total Expenses: $_____

Income Minus Expenses = Your Reserve $_____

appendix 2

marriage principles

1. We will seek to put God first in our lives.

"And He is the head of the body, the church; He is the beginning and the firstborn from among the dead, so that in everything He might have the supremacy."

Colossians 1:18

2. We will pray and work together for spiritual oneness.

"Make every effort to keep the unity of the Spirit through the bond of peace."

Ephesians 4:3

3. We will each take responsibility for our own life and joy in the Lord.

"You have made known to me the path of life; you will fill me with joy in your presence, with eternal pleasures at your right hand."

Psalm 16:11

4. We will practice unconditional love.

"In this same way, husbands ought to love their wives as their own bodies. He who loves his wife loves himself. After all, no one ever hated his own body, but he feeds and cares for it, just as Christ does the church—"

Ephesians 5:28-29

5. We will make the love described in I Corinthians 13 our marriage goal.

"Love is patient, love is kind. It does not envy, it does not boast, it is not proud. It is not rude, it is not self-seeking, it is not easily angered, it keeps no record of wrongs. Love does not delight in evil but rejoices with the truth. It always protects, always trusts, always hopes, always perseveres. Love never fails."

1 Corinthians 13:4-8a

6. We will follow the Biblical Leadership pattern in our marriage.

"Wives, submit to your husbands as to the Lord. For the husband is the head of the wife as Christ is the head of the church, his body, of which he is the Savior. Now as the church submits to Christ, so also wives should submit to their husbands in everything. Husbands, love your wives, just as Christ loved the church and gave himself up for her to make her holy, cleansing her by the washing with water through the word, and to present her to himself as a radiant church, without stain or wrinkle or any other blemish, but holy and blameless. In this same way, husbands ought to love their wives as their own bodies. He who loves his wife loves himself. After all, no one ever hated his own body, but he feeds and cares for it, just as Christ does the church—However, each one of you also must love his wife as he loves himself, and the wife must respect her husband."

Ephesians 5:22-29, 33

7. We will honor our marriage and seek to fulfill each other.

"But at the beginning of creation God 'made them male and female.' 'For this reason a man will leave his father and mother and be united to his wife, and the two will become one flesh.' So they are no longer two, but one. Therefore what God has joined together, let man not separate."

Mark 10:6-9

8. We will give sexual pleasure and satisfaction to each other.

"The husband should fulfill his marital duty to his wife, and likewise the wife to her husband. The wife's body does not belong to her alone but also to her husband. In the same way, the husband's body does not belong to him alone but also to his wife. Do not deprive each other except by mutual consent and for a time, so that you may devote yourselves to prayer. Then come together again so that Satan will not tempt you because of your lack of self-control."
I Corinthians 7:3-5

9. We will cherish our "first love."

"We love because He first loved us."
John 4:19

10. We will be totally open and honest.

"Do not lie to each other, since you have taken off your old self with its practices."
Colossians 3:9

11. We will seek to encourage each other in all ways.

"Therefore encourage one another and build each other up, just as in fact you are doing."
1 Thessalonians 5:11

12. We will treasure spontaneity and set aside time for each other in our relationship.

13. We will not punish each other by being contrary, manipulative or withdrawn.

14. We will learn to deal with anger and frustration in an appropriate and timely manner.

"'In your anger do not sin': Do not let the sun go down while you are still angry."

Ephesians 4:26

15. We will handle our finances together in a responsible manner.

"Give everyone what you owe him: If you owe taxes, pay taxes; if revenue, then revenue; if respect, then respect; if honor, then honor. Let no debt remain outstanding, except the continuing debt to love one another, for he who loves his fellowman has fulfilled the law."

Romans 13: 7-8

16. We will practice good hygiene.

navigating through divorce

31 days journal

navigating through divorce: journal

day 1

*"Trust in Him at all times, O people; **pour out your hearts to Him,** for God is our refuge. 'Selah' [pause and think about that]"*

Psalm 62:8

Write a prayer telling God about how you feel today. Pour your heart out to Him.

navigating through divorce: journal

day 2

*"I will cleanse them from all the sin they have committed against me and will **forgive** all their sins of **rebellion** against me."*

Jeremiah 33:8

Today deal with the past God's way: **repent** [confess and turn from wrong] if you've sinned. Ask God to show you any sin or rebellion—especially in regards to your marriage or divorce. Record what He shows you and then write a prayer thanking God for His forgiveness.

navigating through divorce: journal

day 3

*"Trust in the LORD with all your heart and **lean not on your own understanding**; in all your ways acknowledge him, and he will make your paths straight."*

Proverbs 3:5-6

Today deal with the past God's way: **forgive** your ex-spouse for the hurt you've experienced. Write out the forgiveness steps in chapter 13 and tell God you choose to forgive.

navigating through divorce: journal

day 4

"**Give thanks** in all circumstances, for this is God's will for you in Christ Jesus."

1 Thessalonians 5:18

Today deal with the past God's way: **thank God** for all of it—the parts you liked as well as the painful parts. Write a prayer of thanksgiving below.

navigating through divorce: journal

day 5

"*Whether you turn to the right or to the left, **your ears will hear a voice** behind you, saying, 'This is the way; walk in it.'*"

Isaiah 30:21

Ask God to show you the next steps you are to take—to move forward in your life. Write what He shows you.

navigating through divorce: journal

day 6

"May my cry come before you, O LORD; give me understanding according to your word."

Psalm 119:169

Record the emotions you have been feeling lately and then talk to God about what you have written.

navigating through divorce: journal

day 7

*"Turn your ear to me, come quickly to my rescue; **be my rock** of refuge, a strong fortress to save me."*

Psalm 31:2

The second stage of divorce is a time of *adjustment*—going from being two to being one. Record the main adjustment you are struggling with right now then talk to God about it.

navigating through divorce: journal

day 8

*"But **grow** in the grace and knowledge of our Lord and Savior Jesus Christ. To Him be glory both now and forever! Amen."* 2 Peter 3: 18

The third stage of divorce is a time of *growth* or being stretched. Consider the areas (like spiritually, socially, financially or parentally) you are growing in and record them below. Thank God for this growth.

navigating through divorce: journal

day 9

*"Call to me and **I will answer you and tell you** great and unsearchable things you do not know."*

Jeremiah 33:3

Talk to God today like you would a best friend or a loving father. Shut out distractions and listen to Him. Write what He tells you. He will tell you how much *He loves you and give you direction for your life.*

navigating through divorce: journal

day 10

"*O LORD, **I call to you;** come quickly to me. Hear my voice when I call to You.*"

Psalm 141:1

Record whatever is on your mind today and then talk to God about what you have written.

navigating through divorce: journal

day 11

*"**Delight yourself in the Lord** and He will give you the desires of your heart."*

Psalm 37:4

Smile! God loves you. You are precious to Him. Write how you feel about His love and tell Him the desires of your heart.

navigating through divorce: journal

day 12

"Be pleased, O LORD, to **save me**; O LORD, come quickly to **help me.**"

Psalm 40:13

If you need some extra strength to overcome temptation, negative emotions or wrong behavior today, write your prayer below. God will help you!

navigating through divorce: journal

day 13

"O LORD, I call to You; come quickly to me. Hear my voice when I call to You."

Psalm 141:1

Record whatever is on your mind and then talk to God about what you have written.

navigating through divorce: journal

day 14

"When I was woven together in the depths of the earth, Your eyes saw my unformed body. All the days ordained for me were written in Your book before one of them came to be."

Psalm 139:15-16

God loves you so much that He designed a plan for your life *before* you were born! You have value and worth. Thank Him for creating you, loving you and having a plan for your life.

navigating through divorce: journal

day 15

*"The LORD appeared to us in the past, saying: 'I have loved you with an **everlasting love**; I have drawn you with loving-kindness.'"*

Jeremiah 31:3

Declare out loud: "I am deeply loved by God, completely forgiven because of Jesus, fully pleasing to my Heavenly Father, totally accepted by God and complete in Christ." Record your thoughts and feelings in regards to this verse (Jeremiah 31:3) and declaration.

navigating through divorce: journal

day 16

*"'For I know the **plans** I have for you,' declares the LORD, '**plans** to prosper you and not to harm you, **plans** to give you hope and a future.'"* Jeremiah 29:11

Plans, plans, plans! God has wonderful plans for your life. Write the changes you believe God wants to make in your life—spiritually, psychologically, socially, physically, financially, martially and parentally. Talk to Him about what you write.

navigating through divorce: journal

day 17

"Whatever you do, do it all for the glory of God."
1 Corinthians 10:31

Today make a list of your lifetime goals. Don't stop to think about it; just write everything down. Be specific then consider whether these goals are pleasing to God.

navigating through divorce: journal

day 18

"For we are God's workmanship, created in Christ Jesus to do **good works**, which God prepared in advance for us to do."

Ephesians 2:10

You were created by God. You are His masterpiece and designed to accomplish some very special things. Ask God to reveal the good works you are to walk in today and write down what He shows you.

navigating through divorce: journal

day 19

"For God did not give us a **spirit of timidity [fear]**, but a spirit of power, of love and of self-discipline [sound mind]."

2 Timothy 1:7

List the fears you are battling right now. Declare: "God has not given me a spirit of fear but He has given me His power, love and a sound mind."

navigating through divorce: journal

day 20

"I can do everything through Him who gives me strength."
                                                    Philippians 4:13

Turn your focus off of yourself by focusing on Jesus and others. Ask God to show you someone who is hurting more than you are and help them today. Afterwards write who you helped, what you did and how you felt.

navigating through divorce: journal

day 21

*"Then Peter came to Jesus and asked, 'Lord, how many times shall I **forgive** my brother when he sins against me? Up to seven times?' Jesus answered, 'I tell you, not seven times, but seventy-seven times.'"*

Matthew 18:21-22

Have new offenses toward you taken place? Take the time right now to forgive AGAIN. Be free from unforgiveness. Write out the offense, your feelings (the emotional hurt) and the ramifications (how the offense affected other areas of your life—then pray and forgive.

navigating through divorce: journal

day 22

*"**Let no debt remain** outstanding, except the continuing debt to love one another, for he who loves his fellowman has fulfilled the law."*

Romans 13:8

If you are in debt, take time right now to fill out the monthly budget in appendix 1. Ask God to help you complete the budget and stick to it.

navigating through divorce: journal

day 23

"No temptation *has seized you except what is common to man. And God is faithful; he will not let you be tempted beyond what you can bear. But when you are tempted, he will also provide a way out so that you can stand up under it."*

1 Corinthians 10:13

What temptations are you facing today? Write a prayer thanking God for strength to overcome temptation and His faithfulness to show you the way out.

navigating through divorce: journal

day 24

". . . God has said, 'Never will I leave you; never will I forsake you.'"

Hebrews 13:5

If you are lonely, tell God about it. Thank Him for being with you and ask Him for opportunities to spend time with some good friends.

navigating through divorce: journal

day 25

"Do not be yoked together with unbelievers. For what do righteousness and wickedness have in common? Or what fellowship can light have with darkness?"

2 Corinthians 6:14

Make a list of the qualities you desire in a future spouse. Talk to God about your list.

navigating through divorce: journal

day 26

"Husbands, love your wives, just as Christ loved the church and gave himself up for her"

Ephesians 5:25

God created husbands to be a loving spiritual leader. Write a prayer asking God to help you find that kind of husband or be that kind of husband.

navigating through divorce: journal

day 27

"She [a good wife] brings him [her husband] good, not harm, all the days of her life."

Proverbs 31:12

God created wives to be a loving support. Write a prayer asking God to help you find that kind of wife or be that kind of wife.

navigating through divorce: journal

day 28

"Praise be to the God and Father of our Lord Jesus Christ, the Father of compassion and the God of all comfort, who comforts us in all our troubles, so that we can comfort those in any trouble with the comfort we ourselves have received from God."

2 Corinthians 1:3-4

Thank God for His comfort and ask Him to bring others into your life who will be helped and comforted by what you have experienced and learned.

navigating through divorce: journal

day 29

*"And we know that in all things **God works for the good** of those who love him, who have been called according to his purpose . . . to be conformed to the likeness of his Son, that he might be the firstborn among many brothers."*

Romans 8:28-29

God is using everything you have gone through for good—so you can comfort others and so you will be more like Jesus. In what ways are you closer to God and more like Jesus today than you were before your divorce? Write a prayer of thanksgiving.

navigating through divorce: journal

day 30

*"**Cast all your anxiety** on Him because He cares for you."*
1 Peter 5:7

Give all of your anxieties, all of your worries and all of your concerns to God today. Why? Because He cares for YOU affectionately! As you pray, picture yourself placing all of your burdens into His mighty hands. Leave them there and walk away content.

navigating through divorce: journal

day 31

"If they obey and serve Him, they will spend the rest of their days in prosperity and their years in **contentment.***"*

Job 36:11

Remember: *No* person and *no* situation need to change for you to be contented. That's good news because certain people and situations might *never* change. Write what God has shown you as you have read this book.

(I'd love to know what you write on this page. Please email me: edith.joy.carney@gmail.com)